HENRY JAMES

HENRY JAMES

HENRY JAMES

By

REBECCA WEST

KENNIKAT PRESS, INC./PORT WASHINGTON, N. Y.

HENRY JAMES

First Published in 1916
Reissued in 1968 by Kennikat Press

Library of Congress Catalog Card No: 67-27663

Manufactured in the United States of America

AUTHOR'S NOTE

I wish to acknowledge my indebtedness for help in compiling the bibliography to Mr James B. Pinker, Miss Wilma Meikle, and Messrs Constable; and to Messrs Macmillan for the loan of the New York Edition of the Novels and Tales of Henry James.

R. W.

CONTENTS

I

THE SOURCES

AT various times during the latter half of the eighteenth century there crossed the Atlantic two Protestant Irishmen, a Lowland Scotsman, and an Englishman, and thereby they fixed the character of Mr Henry James' genius. For the essential thing about Mr James was that he was an American; and that meant, for his type and generation, that he could never feel at home until he was in exile. He came of a stock that was the product of culture and needed it as part of its environment. But at the time of his childhood and youth—he was born in 1843—culture was a thing that was but budding here and there in America, in such corners as were not being used in the business of establishing the material civilisation of the new country. The social life of old New York and Boston had its delicacy, its homespun honesty of texture, its austerer sort of beauty; but plainly the American people were too preoccupied by their businesses and professions to devote their money to the embellishment of *salons* or their intelligence to the development of manners. Hawthorne and Emerson and Margaret Fuller and their friends were trying to make a culture against time; but any record of their lives which gives a candid account of how desperately these people had to struggle to make the meanest living shows that the poor American ants were then utterly unable to form the leisured community which is the necessary environment for grasshoppers. "The impression of Emerson's personal history is condensed into the single word Concord," wrote Mr James later, "and all the condensation in the world will not make it rich." There was no blinking the fact that in attempting to set up in this unfinished country Art was like a delicate lady who moves into a house before the plaster is dried on the walls; she was bound to lead an invalid existence.

10

This incapacity of America to supply the colour of life became obvious to Henry and William James, the two charming little boys in tight trousers and brass-buttoned jackets, one of whom grew up to write fiction as though it were philosophy and the other to write philosophy as though it were fiction, at a very early age. It did not escape their infant observation that the ladies and gentlemen who fascinated them by dancing on the tight-rope at Barnum's Museum always bore exotic names, and when they grew older and developed the youthful taste for anecdotic art they found it could be gratified only by such European importations as Thorwaldsen's *Christ and His Disciples*, the great white images of which were ranged round the maroon walls of the New York Crystal Palace, or Benjamin's Haydon's pictures in the Düsseldorf collection in Broadway. And when they grew older still and began to show a fine talent for painting and drawing their unfolding artistic sense found more and more intimations of the wonder of Europe. *A View of Tuscany* that hung in the Jameses' home was pronounced by a friend who had lived much in Italy not to be of Tuscany at all. Colours in Tuscany were softer; but such brightness might be found in other parts of Italy. So Europe was as various as that—a place of innumerable changing glories like a sunrise, but better than a sunrise, inasmuch as every glory was encrusted with the richness of legend.

But most powerful of all influences that made the Jameses rebel against the narrowness of Broadway and the provincial spareness of the old New York, which must have been something like a neat virgin Bloomsbury, was their father. The Reverend Henry James was wasted on young America; it had developed neither the creative stream that would have inspired him nor the intellectual follies that he could slay with that beautiful wit which made him one of the great letter-writers of the world. " Carlyle is the same old sausage, fizzing and sputtering in his own grease, only infinitely *more* unreconciled to the blest Providence which

guides human affairs. He names God frequently and alludes to the highest things as
if they were realities, but all only as for a
picturesque effect, so completely does he
seem to regard them as habitually circum-
vented and set at naught by the politicians."
The man who could write that should
have been a strong and salutary influence
on English culture, and he knew it. It is
probable that when he and his wife paid
what Mr James tells us was their " first (that
is our mother's first) visit to Europe, which
had quite immediately followed my birth,
which appears to have lasted some year and
a half "—the last clause of this sentence is
unfortunate for a novelist famous for his
deliberation—he brought his babies with him
with a solemnity of intention, as if to dip
them in a holy well. Thus it was that the
little Jameses not only bore themselves
proudly through their childhood as became
those who had lived as babies in Piccadilly,
and read *Punch* with a proprietary instinct,
but were also possessed in spirit by something that was more than the discontent

with the flatness of daily life and the desire for a brighter scene that comes to the ordinary child. From their father's preoccupation they gained a rationalised consciousness that America was an incomplete environment, that in Europe there were many mines of treasure which they must find and rifle if they hoped for the health of their minds and the salvation of their souls.

In 1855, when Henry James was twelve, the family yielded to its passion and crossed the Atlantic. The following four years were of immense importance to Mr James, and consequently to ourselves, for he had been born with a mind that received impressions as if they had been embraces and remembered them with as fierce a leaping of the blood; just as his brother William's mind acquired and created systems of thought as joyously as other men like meeting friends and establishing a family. He found London in the main jolly, rather ugly, but comfortable and full of character, just as he had seen it in *Punch*, but here and there detected—

notably on a drive from London Bridge—
black outcrops of Hogarth's London. "It
was a soft June evening, with a lingering
light and swarming crowds, as they then
seemed to me, of figures reminding me of
George Cruikshank's Artful Dodger and his
Bill Sykes and his Nancy, only with the
bigger brutality of life, which pressed upon
the cab, the Early Victorian four-wheeler,
as we jogged over the Bridge, and cropped
up in more and more gas-lit patches for all
our course, culminating, somewhere far to
the west, in the vivid picture, framed by the
cab window, of a woman reeling backward
as a man felled her to the ground with a blow
in the face." He knew Paris, then being
formed by the free flourish of Baron Hauss-
mann into its present splendours of wide
regularity, yet still homely with remnants
of the dusty ruralism of its pre-Napoleonic
state; he saw all the pretty show of the
Second Empire, he stood in the Champs-
Elysées and watched the baby Prince
Imperial roll by to St. Cloud with his escort
of blue and silver *cent-gardes*; and the

Galerie d'Apollon in the Louvre, its floors
gleaming with polished wood, its walls
glowing with masterpieces, and its pro-
portions awesomely interminable and soaring, was the scene of his young imaginative
life. Those were the great places; but there
were also Geneva and Boulogne and Zurich
and Bonn, the differences of which he
savoured, and above all the richness of
desultory contact with arts and persons of
the various countries. He gaped at the
exquisiteness of ugly Rose Chéri at the
Gymnase, copied Delacroix, read *Evan
Harrington* as it came out in *Once a
Week*; was at school with a straight-
nosed boy called Henry Houssaye and a
snub-nosed boy called Coquelin; was
tutored by Robert Thompson, the famous
Edinburgh teacher who was afterwards to
instruct Robert Louis Stevenson and many
other eminent Scots in Jacobite sympathies
as well as the more usual subjects, and by
M. Lerambert whose verse had been praised
by Sainte-Beuve in his *Causeries*. "Impressions," writes Mr James of this period,

" were not merely all right but were the dearest things in the world."

And one must remember that not only were impressions much to young Henry James, they were all he had. His mental life consisted of nothing else. His natural inaptitude for acquiring systematised knowledge was probably intensified by the study of foreign languages entailed by this travel; for if a child spends its time learning several systems of naming things it plainly has less energy to spare for learning systems of arranging things. At any rate his inability to grasp the elements of arithmetic and mathematics led to his removal from the Polytechnic School at Zurich, and was the cause of despair in all his tutors. But most minds, however incapable they may be of following the exact sciences or speculative thought, have some sort of idea of the system of the universe inserted into them by early instruction in one or other of the religious faiths. This unifying influence was refused to Henry James by the circumstance that his father had found certain religious doubts

17

that had almost driven him from the ministry
solved in the works of Swedenborg, which he
found not at all incredible but—as he once
said in a phrase that showed him his son's
own father—fairly " insipid with veracity."
On this foundation of Swedenborgianism he
had built up for himself a religion which was
" nothing if not a philosophy, extraordinarily complex and worked out and original,
intensely personal as an exposition, yet not
only susceptible of application, but clamor-
ous for it, to the whole field of consciousness,
nature and society, history, knowledge, all
human relations and questions, every pulse
of the process of our destiny."   This was no
playground for the young intelligence, so
young Henry James was told to prepare
himself by drinking from such springs as
seemed to him refreshing.   When he was
asked to what church he went he was bidden
by his father to reply that " we could plead
nothing less than the whole privilege of
Christendom, and that there was no com-
munion, even that of the Catholics, even that
of the Jews, even that of the Swedenborgians,

from which we need find ourselves excluded."
He certainly liked to exercise this privilege,
but he admits that " my grounds may have
been but the love of the *exhibition* in general,
thanks to which figures, faces, furniture,
sounds, smells and colours became for me,
wherever enjoyed, and enjoyed most where
most collected, a positive little orgy of the
senses and riot of the mind." Which was
to be expected ; as also was the fact that he
never broke his childish habit of regarding
his father's religion as a closed temple stand-
ing in the centre of his family life, the general
holiness of which he took for granted so
thoroughly that it never occurred to him to
investigate its particulars.

This European visit came to an end in
1859, and William and Henry James spent
the next year or so at Newport studying art
under the direction of their friend John La
Farge, with the result that William painted
extremely well in the style of Manet, and
Henry showed as little ability in this direction as he had shown in any other. In 1861
the Civil War broke out; and had it not

been for an accident the whole character of
Mr James' genius would have been altered.
If he had seen America by the light of burst-
ing shells and flaming forest he might never
have taken his eyes off her again, he might
have watched her fascinated through all
the changes of tone and organisation which
began at the close of the war, he might have
been the Great American Novelist in subject
as well as origin.   But it happened, in that
soft spring when he and every other young
man of the North realised that there was a
crisis at hand in which their honour was
concerned and they must answer Lincoln's
appeal for recruits, that he was one day called
to help in putting out a fire.   In working the
fire-engine he sustained an injury so serious
that he could never hope to share the
Northern glory, that there were before him
years of continuous pain and weakness, that
ultimately he formed a curious and on the
whole mischievous conception of himself. .
For his humiliating position as a delicate and
unpromising student at Harvard Law School
while his younger brothers, Wilky and

Robertson, were officers in the Northern
Army and William was pursuing a brilliant
academic career or naturalising with Agassiz
in South America, seemed a confirmation of
his tutors' opinion that he was an inarticulate
mediocrity who would never be able to take
a hand in the business of life. And so he
worked out a scheme of existence, which he
accepted finally in an hour of glowing resig-
nation when he was returning by steamer to
Newport from a visit to a camp of wounded
soldiers at Portsmouth Grove, in which the
one who stood aside and felt rather than acted
acquired thereby a mystic value, a spiritual
supremacy, which—but this was perhaps a
later development of the theory—would be
rubbed off by participation in action.

It was, therefore, with defiant industry,
with the intention of proving that such as
he was he had his peculiar worth, that he
set to work to become a writer. His first
story was published in *The Atlantic Monthly*
when he was twenty-one, and it was followed
by a number of stories, travel sketches, and
critical essays, some of which have been

reprinted, and a few farces which have not. He also went through a necessary preface of the literary life by reading the proofs of George Eliot's novels before they appeared in the *Atlantic* and reviewing; the profession of literature differs from that of the stage in that the stars begin instead of ending as dressers. In 1869 he went to Europe and, gaining certain impressions that had been inaccessible to him as a child, finally fixed the dye in which his talent was to be immersed for the rest of his life. He stepped for the first time into " a private park of great oaks . . . where I knew my first sense of a matter afterwards, through fortunate years, to be more fully disclosed: the springtime in such places, the adored footpath, the first primroses, the stir and scent of renascence in the watered sunshine and under spreading boughs that were somehow before aught else the still reach of the remembered lines of Tennyson. . . ." He was admitted to the homes of Ruskin, Rossetti, Morris, Darwin, and George Eliot, and allowed to see the wheels go round. But the real significance of this journey to Mr James' genius is the part it played in the last days of his beautiful cousin, Mary Temple. She should have had before her a long career of nobility, for " she was absolutely afraid of nothing she might come to by living with enough sincerity and enough wonder." She pretended not to know that she had been cheated out of this, but as she lay on the death-bed that she would not admit to be even a sick-bed, her eyes were fixed intensely on the progress of her cousin through all the experiences that should have been hers. There came a day when all illusion failed, and she died dreadfully, clinging to consciousness. Her death was felt by Henry and William James as the end of their youth.

That, as Mr James would have said, is the *donnée*. The must was trodden out, it had only to ferment, to be bottled, to be mellowed by time into the perfect wine. There is nothing in all the innumerable volumes that Mr James was to pour out in the next forty-five years of which the intimation is not present in these first adventures.

II

THE INTERNATIONAL SITUATION

IT is no use turning up those first stories that appeared in *The Atlantic Monthly* and *The Galaxy* unless one has formed an affection for the literary personality of Mr James. The image they provoke of the literary prentice bending over his task with the tip of his tongue reflectively protruding like a small boy drawing on his slate, is amusing enough; but they themselves are such pale dreams as might visit a New England spinster looking out from her snuff-coloured parlour on a grey drizzling day. Where there is any richness of effect, as in *The Romance of Certain Old Clothes*, it comes from the influence of Nathaniel Hawthorne. That story, which tells how a girl loved her sister's husband, waited eagerly for her death that she might marry him, and later wheedled from him the key of the chest in which the dead wife had left her finery to await her baby daughter's maturity, is seven-eighths prelude, and the catastrophe, which is the finding of the girl kneeling dead beside the chest with the mark of phantom fingers on her throat, comes with too short and small a report. But in spite of its pitiful construction it is the only one of the dozen stories which Mr James published before his visit to Europe in 1869 that shows any of the imaginative exuberance which one accepts as an earnest of coming genius.

Hawthorne was not altogether a happy influence—it is due to him that Mr James' characters have " almost wailed " their way from *The Passionate Pilgrim* to *The Golden Bowl*—but he certainly shepherded Mr James into the European environment and lent him a framework on which to drape his emotions until he had discovered his own power to build up an imaginative structure. The plot of *The Passionate Pilgrim*, with its American who comes to England to claim a cousin's estate, falls in love with the usurper's sister, is driven from the door, and dies just after the usurper's death has delivered to him all he wants, is very clumsy Hawthorne, but in those days Mr James could not draw normal events and he had to have some medium for expressing his wealth of feeling about England. It is amazing to see how rich that wealth already was, how much deeper than mere pleasure in travel was his delight in the parks and private grandeurs of England; and how, too, a fundamental fallacy was already perverting it to an almost Calvinist distrust of the activities of the present.

" I entered upon life a perfect gentleman," says the American as he sits in Hampton Court. " I had the love of old forms and pleasant rites, and I found them nowhere— found a world all hard lines and harsh lights, without lines, without composition, as they say of pictures, without the lovely mystery of colour. . . . Sitting here, in this old park, in this old country, I feel that I hover on the misty verge of what might have been! I should have been born here, not there; here my makeshift distinctions would have found things they'd have been true of. . . .

26

This is a world I could have got on with beautifully."

There you have the first statement of the persistent illusion, to which he was helped by his odd lack of the historic sense and which confused his estimate of modern life, that the past would have been a happier home for those who like himself loved fastidious living. He had a tremendous sense of the thing that is and none at all of the thing that has been, and thus he was always being misled by such lovely shells of the past as Hampton Court into the belief that the past which inhabited them was as lovely. The calm of Canterbury Close appeared to him as a remnant of a time when all England, bowed before the Church, was as calm; whereas the calm is really a modern condition brought about when the Church ceased to have anything to do with England. He never perceived that life is always a little painful at the moment, not only at this moment but at all moments; that the wine of experience always makes a raw draught when it has just been trodden out from bruised grapes by the pitiless feet of men, that it must be subject to time before it acquires suavity. The lack of this perception matters little in his early work but it is vastly important in shaping his later phases.

There are no such personal revelations in *The Madonna of the Future*, nor anything, indeed, at all characteristic of Mr James. There is beauty in the tale of the American painter who dreams over a model for twenty years, while he and she grow old, and leaves at his death nothing more to show for his dreams than a cracked blank canvas; and the Florentine background is worked on diligently and affectionately. But it is admirable in quite an uncharacteristic way, like a figure picture painted with the utmost brilliance of technique and from perfect models by a painter whose real passion was for landscape. Yet it was only a year later, in *Madame de Mauves*, that Mr James found himself, both his manner and the core of the matter which was to occupy him for the happiest part of his literary life. Euphemia de Mauves, the prim young American who moves languidly through the turfy avenues of the French forest, her faith in decency of living perpetually outraged by her husband's infidelities and his odd demand that she should make him a cuckold so that at least he should not have the discomfort of looking up at her, is the first of the many exquisite women whom Mr James brought into being by his capacity to imagine characters solidly and completely, his perception of the subtle tones of life, and his extreme verbal delicacy. And she is given a still greater importance by the queer twist at the end of the story by which M. de Mauves blows his brains out for no reason at all but that he is hopelessly, helplessly, romantically in love with this cold wife who will be so unreasonable about trifles. Mr James writes her story not only as though he stood upon the Atlantic shores looking eastward at the plight of a compatriot domiciled with lewd men and light women, but also as though he sat in the company of certain gracious men and women of the world who could not get under way with their accomplishment of charm because the grim alien in the corner will keep prodding them with a disapproval as out of place in this salon as a deal plank. Madame de Mauves, in fine, is the first figure invented by Mr James to throw light upon what he called " the international situation."

It took all Mr James' cosmopolitan training to see that there existed an international situation, that the fact that Americans visited Europe constituted a drama. An Englishman who visited Italy did no more than take a look at a more richly coloured order of life that braced him up, as any gay spectacle might have done, to return to his own; his travel was a pleasure, or, at most, if he happened to be a Landor or a Browning, an inspiration. It might reasonably be supposed that the visit to Europe of an American was no greater matter. But Mr James knew that the wealthy American was in the position of a man who has built a comfortable house and has plenty of money over, yet cannot furnish it because furniture is neither made nor sold in his country; until he has crossed the sea to the land where they do make furniture he must sleep and eat on the floor.

" One might enumerate," he writes in those early days, " the items of high civilisation as it exists in other countries, which are absent from the texture of American life, until it should become a wonder what was left. No State, in the European sense of the word, and indeed barely a specific national name. No sovereign, no court, no personal loyalty, no aristocracy. . . ."

There follows a long list, so long as to provoke the " natural remark . . . that if these things are left out everything is left out." And, Mr James goes on to complain, " it takes so many things—such an accumulation of history and custom, such a complexity of manners and types, to form a fund of suggestion for a novelist." He wrote novelist because at the moment he was criticising Hawthorne, but he would certainly have applied his phrase to anyone who desired his life to be not a corduroy track

but a marble terrace with palaces on the one
hand and fair gardens on the other.

Since the pilgrimage for these items of
high civilisation appeared to Europeans—
as innumerable contemporary allusions
show it did—as mere globe-trottings, the
pilgrims themselves were likely to be as mis-
understood. For one thing, although they
were unorganised so far as culture went, they
formed at home a very cohesive moral community. The American women who came
to Europe took for granted that however
people might be habited—people, that is,
whose manners showed them "nice"—and
in whatever frivolous array they might be
flounced and ribboned, they were certain to
wear next their skin the hair-shirt of Puritan
rectitude. The innocent freedoms which
they permitted themselves because they
held this supposition, and the terrifying sur-
mises to which these gave rise in the mind of
the Old World, unaware of the innocence of
the New, made much material for drama.
And more dramatic still was the moment,
which came to so many of the travellers who

formed close personal relationships with Europeans, when they realised that the moral standards to which they had nationally pledged themselves, and which they individually obeyed with extraordinary fidelity, were here regarded as simply dowdy. " Compromise ! " was the cry of Latin and even English society. " Compromise on every and any of the Commandments you like ! Do anything you can, in fact, to rub down those rude angles you present to human intercourse ! " And yet it was not to be deduced that Europe was lax. One had only to look behind the superficial show to see that it had its own religion, perhaps a more terrible religion than any New England ever knew, and that what seemed its laziest pleasures were sometimes its most dreadful rites.

This last conception of Europe is the subject of *Roderick Hudson* (1875). *Roderick Hudson* is not a good book. It throws a light upon the lack of attention given at that period to the art of writing that within a few years of each other two men of great

genius—Thomas Hardy and Henry James—
wrote in their thirties first novels spoilt by
technical blemishes of a sort that the most
giftless modern miss with a subscription to
Mudie's would never commit in her first
literary experiment. *Roderick Hudson* is
wooden, it is crammed with local colour like
a schoolmistress's bedroom full of photographs of Rome, it has a plain boiled suet
heroine called Mary. But its idea is mag-
nificent. An American of fortune takes
Hudson, who has already shown talent as a
sculptor, from his stool in a lawyer's office
in Northampton, Massachusetts, and sets
him up in a studio in Rome. It is the fear
of old Mrs Hudson and of Mary, his fiancée,
that European life will be too soft for him.
But the very opposite occurs; it is he who
is too soft for European life. The business
of art means not only lounging under the
pines of the Villa Ludovisi and chiselling
the noble substance of Carrara marble; it
means also the painful toil of creation, which
demands from the artist an austerer re-
nunciation of every grossness than was ever

expected of any law-abiding citizen of Northampton, which sends a man naked and alone to awful moments which, if he be strong, give him spiritual strength, but if he be weak heap on him the black weakness of neurasthenia. And when that has turned him into a raw, hurt, raging creature he is further snared by the loveliness of Christina Light, who is characteristically European in that her circumstances have not the same clear beauty as her face. She is being hawked over the Continent to find a rich husband by her mother and a Cavaliere who is really her father, and this ugly girl-hood has so corrupted her vigorous spirit that the young American's courtship provokes from her nothing but eccentric favours or perverse insults. After the collapse of his art and his love Roderick falls over a precipice in a too minutely described Switzerland, hurled by a *dénouement* which has inspired Mr James to one of his broadest jokes. In the first edition Roderick, on hearing that, while he has been vexing his benefactor with his moods, that gentleman has been manfully repressing a passion for Mary, exclaims, " It's like something in a novel ! " which Mr James in the definitive edition has altered to, " It's like something in a bad novel ! "

This conception of Europe as a complex organism which would have no use, or only a cruel use, for those bred by the simple organism of America, animates *Four Meetings* (1877), that exquisite short story which came first of all of the many masterpieces that Mr James was to produce. It is the tale of a little schoolmistress who, having long nourished a passion for Europe upon such slender intimations as photographs of the Castle of Chillon, at last collects a sum for the trip, is met at Havre by a cousin, one of those Americans on whom Continental life has acted as a solvent of all decent moral tissues, and is tricked out of her money by his story of a runaway marriage with a Countess; returns to New England hoping to " see something of this dear old Europe yet," and has that hope ironically fulfilled by the descent upon her for life of the said

Countess, who is so distinctly " something of this dear old Europe" that the very sight of her transports the travelled recounter of the story to " some dusky landing before a shabby Parisian *quatrième*—to an open door revealing a greasy ante-chamber, and to Madame, leaning over the banisters, while she holds a faded dressing-gown together and bawls down to the portress to bring up her coffee." It is one of the saddest stories in the world, and one of the cleverest. There is not one of its simple phrases but has its beautiful bearing on the subject, and in the treatment of emotional values one sees that the essays on *French Poets and Novelists* (1878), which for some years he had been sending to America with the excited air of a missionary, were the notes of an attentive pupil. " Detachment" was the lesson that that period preached in its reaction against the George Sand method, whereby the author rolled through his pages locked in an embrace with his subject. We have forgotten its real significance, so frequently has it been used as an excuse for the treatment of emotional situations with encyclopædic detail of circumstance and not a grain of emotional realisation, but here we can recover it. The author's pity for the schoolmistress is never allowed to make his Countess sinister instead of gross, and his sense of the comic in the Countess is never allowed to make the schoolmistress's woe more dreary; the situation stands as solid and has as many aspects as it would have in life.

The American (1877) still holds this view of Europe. Its theme, to quote Mr James in the preface of the definitive edition, is " the situation, in another country and an aristocratic society, of some robust but insidiously beguiled and betrayed, some cruelly wronged compatriot; the point being in especial that he should suffer at the hands of persons pretending to represent the highest possible civilisation and to be of an order far superior to his own." Christopher Newman, the robust compatriot, is such a large, simple, lovable person that the rest of the story leads one to suspect that one may say of Mr James, as he said of Balzac, that " his figures, as a general thing, are better than the use he makes of them." He walks through Europe examining its culture with such an effect on the natives as an amiable buffalo traversing the Galerie d'Apollon might produce upon the copyists of the Louvre, and finally presents himself at the house where he is least welcome in the world, the home of the de Bellegardes, a proud and ancient Royalist family. Thereafter, the novel is an exposition of the way things do not happen. Claire de Cintré, the widowed daughter whom Newman desires to marry, is represented as having above all things beauty of character; but when her family snatches her from him in a frenzy of pride she allows herself to be bundled into a convent with a weakness that would convict of imbecility any woman of twenty-eight. And since her mother and brother had murdered her father by refusing him medicine at a physical crisis, and sustained themselves in the act by the reflection that after all they were only keeping up the good old family tone, one wonders where she got this beauty of character. The child of this damned house might have flamed with a strange fire, but she could not have diffused a rectory lamplight. But the series of inconsistencies of which this is only one leads, like a jolting motor-bus that puts one down at Hampton Court, to an exquisite situation. Newman discovers the secret of the Marquis' murder and intends to publish it as a punishment for the cruel wrong the de Bellegardes have done him, but sacrifices this satisfaction simply because there can be no link—not even the link of revenge—between such as they and such as he. In all literature there is no passage so full of the very passion of moral exaltation as the description of how Newman stands before the Carmelite house in the Rue d'Enfer and looks up at the blank, discoloured wall, behind which his lost lady is immured, then walks back to Notre Dame and there, " the far-away bells chiming off into space, at long intervals, the big bronze syllables of the Word," decides that such things as revenge " were really not his game." So it is with Mr James to the end. The foreground is as often as not red with the blood of slaughtered probabilities; a gentleman at a dinner-party tells the lady on his left (a perfect stranger who never appears again in the story) that some years ago he proposed to the lady in white sitting opposite to them; a curio dealer calls on a lady in Portland Place just to wind up the plot. But the great glow at the back, the emotional conflagration, is always right.

The Europeans (1878) marks the first time when Mr James took the international situation as a joke, and he could joke very happily in those days when his sentence was a straight young thing that could run where it liked, instead of a delicate creature swathed in relative clauses as an invalid in shawls. There is no other book by Mr James which has quite the clear, sunlit charm of this description of the visit of Eugenia, the morganatically married Baroness, and her brother Felix, the Bohemian painter, to their cousins' New England farm. There is nothing at all to

their discredit in the past of these two
graceful young people, but they resemble
Harlequin and Columbine in the instability
of their existence and the sharp line they
draw between their privacy and their
publicity. It appears to them natural that
the private life should be spent largely in
wondering how the last public appearance
went off and planning effects for the next,
a point of view which arouses the worst
suspicions in their cousins, who are accus-
tomed to live as though the sky were indeed
a broad open eye. So Felix has the greatest
difficulty in persuading his uncle, who takes
thirty-two bites to a moral decision, just as
Mr Gladstone took thirty-two bites to a
mouthful, that he is a suitable husband for
his cousin Gertrude ; and poor Eugenia fails
altogether in an environment where a lie
from her lips is not treated as *un petit péché
d'une petite femme*, but remains simply a lie.
The frame of mind this state of affairs
produces in the poor lady is exquisitely
described in a passage which shows her going
wistfully through the house of the man who

did not propose to her because he detected her lie, after a visit to his dying mother.

" Mrs Acton had told Eugenia that her waiting-woman would be in the hall to show her downstairs; but the large landing outside her door was empty, and Eugenia stood there looking about. . . . She passed slowly downstairs, still looking about. The broad staircase made a great bend, and in the angle was a high window, looking westward, with a deep bench, covered with a row of flowering plants in curious old pots of blue China-ware. The yellow afternoon light came in through the flowers and flickered a little on the white wainscots. Eugenia paused a moment; the house was perfectly still, save for the ticking, somewhere, of a great clock. The lower hall stretched away at the foot of the stairs, half covered over with a large Oriental rug. Eugenia lingered a little, noticing a great many things. ' *Comme c'est bien !* ' she said to herself; such a large, solid, irreproachable basis of existence the place seemed to her to indicate. And then she reflected that Mrs Acton was soon to withdraw from it. The reflection accompanied her the rest of the way downstairs, where she paused again, making more observations. The hall was extremely broad, and on either side of the front door was a wide, deeply-set window, which threw the shadows of everything back into the house. There were high-backed chairs along the wall and big Eastern vases upon tables, and, on either side, a large cabinet with a glass front and little curiosities within, dimly gleaming. The doors were open—into the darkened parlour, the library, the dining-room. All these rooms seemed empty. Eugenia passed along and stopped a moment on the threshold of each. '*Comme c'est bien !*' she murmured again; she had thought of just such a house as this when she decided to come to America. She opened the front door for herself—her light tread had summoned none of the servants—and on the threshold she gave a last look. . . ."

That is the pure note of the early James, like a pipe played carefully by a boy. It sounds as beautifully in *Daisy Miller*, that short novel which, though it deals with conditions peculiar to a small section of

Continental life forty years ago, will strike each new generation afresh as sad and lovely. Daisy, who is like one of those girls who smile upon us from the covers of American magazines, glaringly beautiful and healthy but without the "tone" given by diligent study of the grace of conduct, comes to Europe and plays in its sunshine like a happy child. She wants to go to the Castle of Chillon, so she accepts the escort for the afternoon of a young American who is staying at the same hotel; she likes to walk in the Pincian, so she takes a stroll there one afternoon with a certain liquid-eyed Roman. The woman who does a thing for the sake of the thing in itself is always suspected by society, and the American colony, which professes the mellow conventions of Europe with all its own national crudity, accuses her of vulgarity and even lightness. They talk so bitterly that when the young American, who is half in love with Daisy, finds her viewing the Colosseum by moonlight with the Roman, he leaps to the conclusion that she is a disreputable woman.

Why he does so is not quite clear, since surely it is the essential thing about a disreputable woman that her evenings are not free for visits to the Colosseum. Poor Daisy takes in part of his meaning and, saying in a little strange voice, " I don't care whether I get Roman fever or not!" goes back to her hotel and dies of malaria. And the young American, "staring at the raw protuberance among the April daisies" in the Protestant cemetery, learns from the Roman's lips that Daisy was " most innocent."

It is a lyric whose beauty may be measured by the attention which, in spite of its tragedy, it everywhere provoked. It was interesting to note how often in the obituary notices of Mr James it was said that he had never attained popularity, for it shows how soon London forgets its gifts of fame. From 1875 to 1885 (to put it roughly) all England and America were as captivated by the clear beauty of Mr James' work as in the nineties they were hypnotised by the bright-coloured beauty of Mr Kipling's art. On London staircases everyone turned to look at the American with the long, silky, black beard which, I am told by one who met him then, gave him the appearance of " an Elizabethan sea captain." But for all the exquisiteness of *Daisy Miller* there were discernible in it certain black lines which, like the dark veining in a crocus that foretells its decay, showed that this was a loveliness which was in the very act of passing. The young American might have been so worked upon by his friends that he could readily believe his Daisy a light woman, but he need not have manifested his acceptance of this belief by being grossly rude to her and by reflecting that if "after Daisy's return there had been an exchange of jokes between the porter and the cab-driver . . . it had ceased to be a matter of serious regret to him that the little American flirt should be ' talked about ' by low-minded menials." When one remembers the grave courtesy with which Christopher Newman treated Mlle Noémie Nioche, the little French drab who called herself *un esprit libre*, it is plain that we are no longer dealing with the same Mr James. The Mr James we are to deal with henceforth had ceased to be an American and had lost his native reactions to emotional stimuli. He was becoming a European and for several years to come was to spend his time slowly mastering its conventions; which means that he was learning a new emotional language.

The first works he produced when he was at once a finished writer and only the cocoon of a European, present the paradoxical appearance of being perfect in phrase and incredibly naive in their estimates of persons and situations. *The Pension Beaurepas* (1879), that melancholy tale of the ailing old American whose wife and daughter have dragged him off on an expensive trip to Europe, while ruin falls on his untended business in New York, has its tone of pathos spoiled by extraordinarily cold-blooded and, to women of to-day, extremely unsavoury discussions of how a girl ought to behave if she wants to be married. *The Siege of London* (1883), which

is the story of a Texan adventuress of
many divorces who marries into an English
county family, fails to produce the designed
effect of outrage, because the adventuress is
the only person who shows any signs of
human worth, and the life which she is
supposed to have violated by her marriage
is suggested simply by statements that the
people concerned had titles and lived in
large houses. In *Pandora* (1884), which
describes a German diplomat's amazement
that an unmarried girl can be a social success
in America, we feel as bored as we would if
we were forced to listen to the exclamations
of a dog-fancier on finding that a Pekingese
with regular features had got a prize at a
dog show. In *Lady Barbarina* (1884),
which tells how a peer's daughter who
marries an American millionaire refuses to
live in America, the American picture is
painted with the flatness of a flagging interest, and we suspect Mr James of taking
English architecture as an index of English
character; he had still to grasp the para-
dox that the people who live in the solidities

of Grosvenor Square are the best colonising
and seafaring stock in the world. In *The
Reverberator* (1888), wherein an American
girl guilelessly prattles to a newspaper
correspondent about the affairs of her
French fiancé's family and is cast out by
them when he publishes her prattlings in the
States, we seem to see the international
situation slowly fading from Mr James'
immediate consciousness. In turning over
its pages we see the author sitting down
before a pile of white paper and finely in-
scribing it with memories of past contacts
with Americans; we do not see him enter-
ing his study with traces still on his lips of a
smile provoked in the street outside by the
loveliness and innocent barbarism of his
compatriots. In those days he had lost
America and had not yet found Europe, but
he was to find it very soon. In *A London
Life* (1889), the tale of an innocent American
girl who comes over to live with her sister
and her aristocratic English husband, and
stands appalled at their debts, their de-
baucheries, their infidelities, he has rendered

beautifully the feeling caused by ill lives when led in old homes of elmy parks and honourable histories. It is a sense of disgust such as comes to the early-rising guest who goes into a drawing-room in the morning and finds last night's coffee-cups and decanters and cigarette ends looking dreadful in the sunlight. The house is being badly managed; it will go to rack and ruin. That is an aspect of England; but the American onlooker is just a clean-minded little thing that might have bloomed anywhere, and all references to her Americanness are dragged in with an effort. It is plain that he had lost all his love for the international situation.

That Mr James continued to write about Americans in Europe long after their common motive and their individual adventures had ceased to excite his wonder or his sympathy, was the manifestation of a certain delusion about his art which was ultimately to do him a mischief. He believed that if one *knew* a subject one could write about it; and since there was no

aspect of the international situation with
which he was not familiar, he could not see
why the description of these aspects should
not easily make art. The profound truth
that an artist should feel passion for his
subject was naturally distasteful to one
who wanted to live wholly without violence
even of the emotions; a preference for
passionless detachment was at that date
the mode in French literature, which was
the only literature that he studied with any
attention. The de Goncourts, Zola, and
even de Maupassant thought that an artist
ought to be able to lift any subject into art
by his treatment, just as an advertising
agent ought to be able to " float " any
article into popularity by his posters. But
human experience, which includes a realisation of the deadness of most of the de Goncourts' and Zola's productions, proves the
contrary. Unless a subject is congenial to
the character of the artist the subconscious
self will not wake up and reward the busy
conscious mind by distributions of its
hoarded riches in the form of the right word,

the magic phrase, the clarifying incident.
Why are books about ideas so commonly bad,
since the genius of M. Anatole France and
Mr Wells have proved that they need not be
so, if it be not that the majority of people
reserve passion for their personal relationships and therefore never " feel " an idea
with the sensitive finger-tips of affection ?

The absence of this necessary attitude to
his subject explains in part the tenuity of
Mr James' later novels on the international
situation ; but there is also another element
that irritates present-day readers and makes
the texture of the life represented seem poor.
That element, which is not peculiar to Mr
James, but is a part of the social atmosphere
of his time, is the persistent presentation of
woman not as a human but as a sexual
being. One can learn nothing of the
heroine's beliefs and character for the
hullabaloo that has been set up because she
has come in too late or gone out too early
or omitted to provide herself with that
figure of questionable use—for the dove-like
manners of the young men forbid the

thought that she was there to protect the girl from assault, and the mild tongues of the young ladies make it unlikely that the duel of the sexes was then so bitter that they required an umpire—the chaperon. It appears that the young woman of that period could get through the world only by perpetually jumping through hoops held up to her by society, a method of progression which was more suited to circus girls than to persons of dignity, and which sometimes caused nasty falls. There is nothing more humiliating to women in all fiction than the end of *A London Life*, where the heroine, appalled at having been left in an opera box alone with a young man, turns to him and begs him, although she knows well that he does not love her, to marry her and save her good name. Purity and innocence are excellent things, but a world in which they have to be guarded by such cramping contrivances of conduct is as ridiculous as a heaven where the saints all go about with their haloes protected by mackintosh covers.

III

TRANSITION

WASHINGTON SQUARE (1881), Mr James' first important work that does not deal with the international situation, is a work of great genius. Into the small mould of the story of how a plain and stupid girl was jilted by a fortune-hunter when he discovered that she would be disinherited by her contemptuous father on her marriage, Mr James concentrated all the sense which he had absorbed throughout his childhood of the simple, provincial life which went on behind the brown stone of old New York. It has in it a wealth of feeling that does not seem to have originated with Mr James, just as an old wives' tale told over and over again by the fireside becomes charged with a synthetic emotion derived from the comments and expressions of innumerable auditors; and one may surmise that Catherine's tragedy was first presented to him as an item of local gossip, sympathetically discussed by his charming New York cousins and friends. Certainly the tale of this dull girl, who was " twenty years old before she treated herself, for evening wear, to a red satin gown trimmed with gold fringe," and progressed by such clumsinesses through a career of which the only remarkable facts were that " Morris Townsend had trifled with her affection, and that her father had broken its spring," is consecrated by an element of pity which was afterwards signally to disappear from Mr James' work.

The book so beautifully expresses the woe of all those people to whom nothing ever happens, who are aware of the gay challenge of life but are prevented by something leaden in their substance from responding, that one is not surprised to find that like most good stories about inarticulate people —like *Une Vie* and *Un Cœur Simple*—it is written with the most deliberate cunning. The story is evoked according to Turgeniev's method of calling his novels out of the inchoate real world; and what that is had better, since Mr James had been using it with increasing power since *Roderick Hudson*, be stated in his own words.

" I have always fondly remembered a remark that I heard fall years ago from the lips of Ivan Turgeniev in regard to his own experience of the usual origin of the fictive picture. It began for him almost always with the vision of some person or persons, who hovered before him, soliciting him, as the active or passive figure, interesting him and appealing to him just as they were and by what they were. He saw them, in that fashion, as *disponibles*, saw them subject to the chances, the complications of existence, and saw them vividly, but then had to find for them the right relations, those that would most bring them out; to imagine, to invent and select and piece together the situations most useful and favourable to the sense of the creatures themselves, the complications they would be most likely to produce and to feel.

" ' To arrive at these things is to arrive

at my " story," ' he said, ' and that's the way I look for it. The result is that I'm often accused of not having " story " enough. I seem to myself to have as much as I need—to show my people, to exhibit their relations with each other; for that is all my measure. If I watch them long enough I see them come together, I see them *placed*, I see them engaged in this or that act and in this or that difficulty. How they look and move and speak and behave, always in the setting I have found for them, is my account of them—of which I dare say, alas, *que cela manque souvent d'architecture. . . .* ' "

And as regards the statement in prose of the conception thus formed it is plain that, although Mr James had formed his irrational dislike of Flaubert many years before, it was that great master who had taught him his art of rubbing down the too brilliant phrase to tone with the quiet harmony of the whole, of obliterating the exotic effect that would compromise the lorn simplicity of the subject. This masterly use of technical resource to unfold an idea whose beauty would to a lesser artist have seemed hopelessly sheathed in obscurity, makes *Washington Square* the perfect termination to Mr James' first period of genius.

It was unfortunately quite definitely a termination; for until ten years had passed Mr James was doomed to produce no work which was not to have the solidity of its characters and the beauty of its prose rendered slightly ridiculous by its lack of purpose and unity. In those days, when the international theme was slipping from Mr James' grasp and he was looking round for another, one could no more expect him to produce work completely and serenely formed by the imagination than one could ask an author to continue his industry on a journey from Paris to Madrid, with the jolting of the train destroying his physical calm and the new land crying for his attention at the carriage window. For Mr James was literally travelling all through the eighties; he was touring either the countries of Europe with his body or the art of Europe with his mind. It was his intention to find that intellectual basis without which, his blood and upbringing assured him, he would be unable to use his genius with noble or permanent results.

How difficult this search was to be, and yet how ultimately fruitful, can be judged from *A Little Tour in France* (1884). That is one of the happiest and sunniest travel books in all literature. *Cœlum non animum mutant qui trans mare currunt*; but Mr James did, and it is as pleasant to see his intelligence sunning itself on the hot Latin soil, fresh and cool as though he had not years of the creative struggle behind him and years more to come, as it is to see a lizard crawl from the crevice of a Provençal rock and play among the tufts of rosemary. Yet whenever Mr James has to note some detail in his description of French towns which refers to the life which has formed them, the reader's fury mounts. It is horrible that his references to the Franco-Prussian War should be faintly jocular, and one burns with shame for them until one comes to an amazing sentence about the French Revolution, in which it is plainly implied that the rightness and necessity of that declaration of the principle of freedom are still debatable questions. One perceives with relief that he said these things because, as one guessed in *The Passionate Pilgrim*, his strong sight of the thing that is was accompanied by blindness to the thing that has been. He did not know whether the Franco-Prussian War was horrible or not, because he had been out of Europe when it raged; and because he had not been born at the time he could no more speak well of the French Revolution than he could propose for his club a person whom he had never met. And for the same reason he failed to envisage the Roman Empire save as a source of agreeable ruins which, since he did not understand the spirit that built them, he imagined might have been made still more agreeable. Their vastness did not impress him as the merging-point of the geological record and history, but stirred in him that benevolence which is often aroused by clumsy largeness. He patted the Roman

Theatre at Arles as though it were Jumbo
at the Zoo, and remarked, quite in the
manner of Horace Walpole, that the pave-
ment of coloured marble " gives an idea of
the *elegance* of the interior " ; but the arena
at Nîmes and that vast, high, yellow aque-
duct, whose three tiers appal the valley of
the Gardon, were too much for him, and he
pronounced them " not at all *exquisite.*"
The man who could write those phrases was
incapable of forming a philosophy, for no
man can fully understand his kind unless he
have a revelation of old Rome and perceive
in its works a record of the pride men felt
in serviceable labour for the State. And
yet what, in this particular case, did all
that matter? What need was there for
Mr James to know anything but that ink
makes black, expressive marks on paper,
when he could tell so exquisitely how the
Château de Chenonceaux sends out its
white galleries across the clear water of
the Cher, how the crenellated ramparts of
the Château d'Amboise look down over
hanging gardens to the far-shining Loire,

and with what peculiar wonder Carcassonne, Aigues-Mortes and all the other towns with lovely names, glow in the clear bright light of France? It was enough that there was no beauty on earth that could daunt his power of description.

The record of his mental wanderings is not quite so happy. Mr James has an immense prestige as critic, but a certain sentence that occurred more than once in his obituary notices made it doubtful whether this does not merely mean that people have run their eyes over the titles of Mr James' essays and have accepted the fact that he dealt with authors rarely read by the British as a guarantee of their rareness of merit. That it should be reverently remarked on that most solemn occasion that Flaubert was Mr James' adored master, when he had written more than one exquisitely feline essay to delicately convey what a fluke it was that this fellow who panted under his phrase like a bricklayer under his hod should have produced *Madame Bovary*, is just such an ironic happening as

he would have liked to be introduced into
one of his humorous studies of the literary
life. Such intimations make one guess
that the homage which England loves to
pay to the unread is responsible for half Mr
James' reputation as a critic; and probably
he owed the other half to the gratitude of
his readers for a pleasure which is un-
doubtedly given by his critical writings, but
which nevertheless does not prove them
great criticism. It is true that *French Poets
and Novelists* are the best reviews ever
written, and that it is good to listen to the
old author gossiping in *Notes on Novelists*
(1914) about the authors he had known long
ago and to watch him tracing, with all his
supreme genius for detecting personality,
the imprint of dead masters on the fading
surface of old work. But he is always
entirely lacking in that necessary element
of great criticism, the capacity for universal
reference. The eye that judges a work of
art should have surveyed the whole human
field, so that it can tell from what clay this
precious thing was made, in what crafts-

man's cot that trick of fashioning was
learned, what natural beauty suggested to
the creative impulse this appropriate form,
what human institution helped or hindered
its making. Of that general culture Mr
James was so deficient that he was capable
of inserting in quite an intelligent essay on
Théophile Gautier this amazing sentence:
" Even his æsthetic principles are held with
a good-humoured laxity that allows him,
for instance, to say in a hundred places the
most delightfully sympathetic and pictorial
things about the romantic or Shakespearean
drama, and yet to describe a pedantically
classical revival of the *Antigone* at Münich
with the most ungrudging relish." And
while this ignorance was perpetually blind-
ing him to the purpose of many fair artistic
structures his literary power was perpetually betraying him into the graceful and
forceful publication of his blindness. Long
after one has forgotten all the deliverances
of critics with greater wisdom but less craft
of phrase, one remembers his extraordinary opinion that Flaubert's *La Tentation*

de Saint Antoine, that book which will appeal in every generation to those who have been visited by the angel of speculative thought, which is not only itself a beautiful growth but has borne beautiful fruit in *Thaïs,* is merely " strange" and has no more reference to life than the gimcrack Eastern Pavilion at an Exposition. And he lacked, moreover, that necessary attribute of the good critic, the power to bid bad authors to go to the devil. There are certain Victorian works of art which, however much esteemed by the many, are no more matter for criticism than a pair of elastic-sided boots; yet there is a paper in *Essays in London* (1893) in which Mr James talks of " the numbers of sorts of distinction, the educated insight, the comprehensive ardour of Mrs Humphry Ward. . . ." It recalls that the art which he privately cultivated was courtesy, but it suggests that his criticism was bound to consist for the most part of just such pleasant foot-notes to the obvious as *Partial Portraits* (1888) which, with the exception of some

interesting personal recollections of Turgeniev, tell us nothing more startling than
that de Maupassant wrote a hard prose and
that Daudet was a Provençal.

How greatly he needed the intellectual
basis which he found in none of these re-
searches becomes increasingly plain in each
novel that he published during this period.
The Portrait of a Lady (1881) is given a
superficial unity by the beauty of its
heroine; on the first reading one cannot
take one's eyes off the clear gaze that
Isabel Archer levels at life. As she moves
forward to meet the world, holding her
fortune in hand without avarice yet very
carefully, lest she should buy anything
gross with it, one thinks that there never
was a heroine who deserved better of life.
" She spent half her time in thinking of
beauty, and bravery, and magnanimity;
she had a fixed determination to regard
the world as a place of brightness, of free
expansion, of irresistible action; she thought
it would be detestable to be afraid or
ashamed. She had an infinite hope that

she would never do anything wrong.'' One
is glad to see that the girl has the most
wonderful friend, a woman who is at once
the most flexible *femme du monde* and the
freshest and most candid soul; and among
the kindnesses this friend does her is her
introduction to a certain Tuscan villa that
looks down on the valley of the Arno, where
on a mossy stone bench tangled with wild
roses there sits Gilbert Osmond, a gentleman of great dignity who has been too
fine to partake in the common struggle
and so lives in honest poverty, with his
daughter Pansy, a little girl from whose
character conventual training has removed
every attribute save whiteness and sweetness, so that she lies under life like a fine
cloth on a sunny bleaching-green. Here,
of all places in the world, she is least likely
to meet the jealousy and falseness and
cruelty which were the only things she
feared, and so she marries Osmond in the
happy faith that henceforth nothing will
be admitted to her life save nobility. But
all her marriage brings the girl is evidence

of increasing painfulness that her friend is
a squalid adventuress who has preserved
her appearance of freshness as carefully as
a strolling musician his fiddle, in order that
she might charm such honest fools as Isabel;
that Osmond has withdrawn from the
world, not because he is too fine for it, but
because he is a hating creature, and hates
the world as he now hates his wife; that
Pansy is the illegitimate child of these two,
and her need of a dowry the chief reason
why Osmond has married Isabel. It is a
tale which would draw tears from a re-
viewer, and yet the conduct invented for
Isabel is so inconsistent and so suggestive
of the nincompoop, and so clearly proceed-
ing from a brain whose ethical world was
but a chaos, that it is a mistake to subject
the book to the white light of a second reading. When we are told that Isabel married
Osmond because " there had been nothing
very delicate in inheriting seventy thousand
pounds, and she hoped he might use her
fortune in a way that might make her
think better of it and would rub off a certain

grossness attaching to the good luck of an unexpected inheritance," we feel that this is mere simpering; for there could be nothing less delicate than to marry a person for any reason but the consciousness of passion. And the grand climax of her conduct, her return to Osmond after the full revelation of his guilt has come to augment her anguish at his unkindness, proves her not the very paragon of ladies but merely very ladylike. If their marriage was to be a reality it was to be a degradation of the will whose integrity the whole book is an invitation to admire; if it was to be a sham it was still a larger concession to society than should have been made by an honest woman. Yet for all the poor quality of the motives which furnish Isabel's moral stuffing, *The Portrait of a Lady* is entirely successful in giving one the sense of having met somebody far too radiantly good for this world.

While that novel reminds one, in the way it " comes off," of a sum in which the right answer is got by wrong working, *The*

Bostonians (1886) reminds one of a foolish song set to a good tune in the way it fails to "come off." The beauty of the writing is so great that there are descriptions of the shabby petticoats of a pioneer, or the vestibule in a mean block of flats, that one would like to learn by heart, so that one might turn the phrases over in the mind when one wants to hear the clinking of pure gold. And the theme, the aptness of young persons possessed of that capacity for contagious enthusiasm which makes the good propagandist to be exploited by the mercenary and to deteriorate under the strain of public life, is specially interesting to our generation. Few of us there are who have not seen with our own eyes elderly egoists building up profitable autocracies out of the ardour of young girls, or fierce advocates of the brotherhood of man mellowing into contemplative emptiers of pint-pots. But, just as the most intellectual conversation may be broken up by the continued squeal of a loose chimney-cowl, so this musical disclosure of fine material is interrupted past any reader's patience by a nagging hostility to political effort. This is not so disgraceful to Mr James as it might seem, for it is simply the survival of an affectation which was forced upon the cultured American of his youth. The pioneers who wanted to raise the small silvery song of art had to tempt their audiences somehow from the big brass band of America's political movements; and so straining was this task that even Emerson, who vibrated to the chord of reform as to no other, was sometimes vexed into such foolish inquiries as " Does he not do more to abolish slavery who works all day in his own garden than he who goes to the abolition meetings and makes a speech ? " It was just one of the results of Mr James' condition at this period that he presented to the world so deliberately and so vividly, and with such an air of feeling, what was no more than the misty reflection of some dead men's transitory irritations.

Politics play a very great part, and in the

same sense, in *The Princess Casamassima*
(1886), but it is the peculiar magic of that
strange book which is at once able and dis-
traught, wild and meticulous, that in it all
perversities are somehow transmuted into
loveliness. It is one of the big jokes in
literature that it was the writer who among
all his contemporaries held the most
sophisticated view of his art, who prided
himself that on him there gleamed no
drop of the dew of naïvetê, that brought
back to fiction the last delicious breath of
the time when even the best books ran on
like this: "It happened that one dark
and stormy night in March I, Sebastian
Melmoth, was traversing the plain of La
Mancha. . . . 'Have at you!' cried the
guard. . . . 'Seat yourself,' said the
stranger, signing to his Hindu attendant
that the bodies should be removed, and com-
mencing to cleanse the blood from his sword
with a richly embroidered handkerchief,
'and I will tell you the story of my
life.'" There is always something doing
in *The Princess Casamassima*, and it is

usually something great, and as a rule it is doing it quite on its own. As a portal to the disordered tale there stands one of the finest short stories in the world; how Miss Pynsent, the shabby little dressmaker who has brought up Hyacinth, the bastard child of a French work-girl now in Millbank for the murder of the peer who betrayed her, is suddenly bidden to bring the boy to his mother's prison deathbed, and how the poor woman drags him up to the brown, window-less walls, the vast blank gate, the looming corridors infused with sallow light, is such a study of the way the institutions devised by man in the interests of justice and order make a child's soul scream, that the reader will for ever after think a great deal less of Pip's adventures on the marshes in *Great Expectations*. Dickens could never have suffused his story with so exquisite and so relevant an emotional effect as the aching of poor Miss Pynsent's heart over this rough introduction of her cherished lamb to the horrible; nor could he have invented that wonderful moment when the child turns from the ravenous embrace of the wasted and disfigured stranger with, "I won't kiss her; Pinnie says she stole a watch!" at which the murderess screams, "*Ah! quelle infamie!* I never stole anything!" and the wardress says with dignity: "I'm sure you needn't put more on her than she has by rights," to which the poor virgin, quite unable to understand the peculiar cachet attaching to a *crime passionel*, cries contritely, "Mercy, more! I thought it so much less!"

And from this portal the book goes on to incidents and persons not less exquisite but still disconcertingly mere portals. It is as though in a mad dream one found oneself passing through the arch in the mellow redness of Hampton Court and straightway emerged on the colonnade of St Paul's, through whose little swing-doors one surprisingly stepped to the prim front of Kensington Palace. There is M. Poupin, the exiled Communist who cannot communicate with the world, or the moustached female companion with whom he dwells in a scrupulously unmarried state, save by platitudes concerning the social organisation: " I'm suffering extremely, but we must all suffer so long as the social question is so abominably, so iniquitously neglected," is his way of intimating a sore throat. There is poor Lady Aurora Langrish, the aristocratic precursor of the sad Miss Huxtables in *The Madras House* : " My father isn't rich, and there's only one of us, Eva, married, and we're not at all handsome. . . . They go into the country all the autumn, all the winter, when there's no one here (except three or four millions) and the rain drips, drips, drips from the trees in the big dull park where my people live, and nothing to do but to go out with three or four others in mackintoshes. . . ." There is dry old Mr Vetch who plays the fiddle in the orchestra at night and fills all the rest of the empty day with love for Hyacinth; and there is Captain Sholto, the Piccadilly swell; and Miss Hennings, the sales-lady, and half-a-dozen admirable others casually affixed by the stretched string of circum-

stance or the glue of coincidence. And quite
the preciousest " piece " in the collection is
the account of how the Princess Casamassima, who is Christina Light of *Roderick
Hudson*, grown to perilous maturity of beauty
and perversity, calls young Hyacinth to her
country house, and there in the beechy park
and flowery lanes makes him talk of the plots
against the rich which later are to cause his
death, and brings him nearer to it by lifting
a face wonderfully pale and pure with
enthusiasm. It is so like that Titian in the
Prado which shows, against a window looking on a park where lovers walk in golden
air under silver poplars, Venus lying on a
satin couch while a young man makes
music for her at an organ; her eyes are
softly intent, and the youth thinks she is
suspended over the world in his music, but
really she is brooding on the whiteness of
his skin beneath his black beard. That likeness suggests that *The Princess Casamassima*
should be taken, not as a novel, but as the
small, fine picture gallery that Mr James
thought fit to add to his mental palace,

already so rich in mere sane living rooms.

It is unpleasant to travel in a runaway motor-car, even if it ultimately spills one into a rose-garden, and when Mr James produced a picture gallery when he had intended a grave study of social differences, he was in much that case. But already in *The Author of Beltraffio* (1884) he had shown his awareness of a movement which had started with the intention of destroying both Christian morality and rationalism, and otherwise making us fearfully gay, and which actually achieved the slight mitigation of the offensiveness of plumbers' shop windows and the recovery by Mr Henry James of control over his machine. That story is not one of Mr James' best; the author makes his readers regard his scene through so small a peephole that even the characters who are to be conceived as above all retiring have to come grossly near if their audience is to make anything of the drama at all. The theme is that an author's wife who considers her husband's

books objectionable lets her child die rather
than that he should grow up in the companionship of one so utterly without reserve; yet, since the tale is told by a total
stranger who is visiting them for the week-
end, she has necessarily to behave with a
lack of reserve that makes her imputed
motive incredible. The special value of
the story lies in the moments when the
author of *Beltraffio*, whose affectation of a
velveteen coat and a remote foreign air
makes us desire to scream out to the week-
end visitor that he is being fooled, and this
is no writer but an artistic photographer,
remarks with some complacency that to
the conventional he appears "no better
than an ancient Greek" and professes a
thirst for "the cultivation of beauty without reserve or precautions." Our happy
generation cannot understand these phrases
which doubtless had their salutary meaning
for that distant day when England fed herself on so low a diet that *Jude the Obscure*
seemed to her a maddening draught. But
they interest us by showing that even Mr

James, who ordinarily turned aside with so chill a wince from the ridiculous, had exposed his consciousness to the æsthetic movement which had been remotely engendered by Leigh Hunt's Cockney crow of joy at Italy and afterwards fostered by Ruskin as one of his wild repartees to the railway train, and which was then being given the middle-class touch by Oscar Wilde.

We feel surprised at Mr James' cognisance of anything so second-rate as this Decadent Movement of the late eighties and early nineties, because most of us basely judge it by its lack of worldly success instead of by its moral mission. The elect of the movement, if one delves in the memory of older Londoners, were certainly silly young men who were careful about the laundering of their evening shirts and who tried to introduce the tone of public-school life into ordinary society. And it is true that for all their talk of art they produced nothing but one good farce and a cartload of such weak, sweet verse as schoolgirls copy into exercise-

books, and that from this small effort they
sank exhausted down to prison, drink,
madness, suicide; and struck whatever other
notes there be in the descending scale of
personal disgrace. And yet, for all its
fruitlessness, that prattle about art gave
them a valid claim on our respect. Never
had beauty been so forgotten; style was
poisoned at the fount of thought by Carlyle, whose sentences were confused dis-
asters like railway accidents, and by Herbert
Spencer, who wrote as though he were the
offspring of two *Times* leaders; among
novelists only Robert Louis Stevenson loved
words, and he had too prudent a care to
water down his gruel to suit sick England's
stomach; and in criticism Andrew Lang,
who had admired Scott and Dickens in his
schooldays and was not going to let himself
down by admiring anybody nearer his own
generation, greeted every exponent of the
real with a high piercing northern sneer.
It was of inestimable value that it should be
cried, no matter in how pert a voice, that
words are jewels which, wisely set, make by

their shining mental light. That the cry
could not save the young men who raised it,
bore out their contention of the time's need
for it; if they, seeking new beauty, could
but celebrate the old dingy sins of towns, it
showed in what a base age they had been
bred. And if they could not save themselves they saved others. Arnold Bennett
and H. G. Wells set off in the nineties in a
world encouragingly full of talk about good
writing. Conrad, mouthing his difficult
strange tales about the sea, found an
audience that would sit hushed. And in
the brain of one who, being then between
forty and fifty years of age, might have been
thought inaccessible to new conceptions of
the art that had for so long preoccupied him,
there passed important thoughts.

" That idea I picked up when I corrected
George Eliot's proofs, oh! so long ago!"
one can imagine Mr James saying, "that
idea that art must be ballasted by didactic-
ism can't be true for me. I've fined it
down, in my reading of the French, to an
opinion that the artist should use his fancy

work to decorate useful articles; but still it isn't true for me. For I must, before I can decorate them, make the useful articles of thought my own, and they are just the one thing that for all my mental wealth I can't acquire. I see them often enough in the shop-windows—the moral and political and philosophical problems so prodigiously produced by my age—and many times have tried the door, but to my touch it never opens, so I have to describe them as I see them through the glass, without having felt or known them with the intimacy of possession! It's true I did once deal with a situation in the history of two peoples, but I see now that in its international character there was an intimation that it was the last with which I should ever effectively concern myself. For I'm destructively not national; my mind is engraved with the sights and social customs of half-a-dozen countries, and with the deep traditions of not one, and how can I deal deeply with the conduct of a people when I haven't a notion of the quality or quantity of the traditions which are,

after all, its mainspring? It seems to me
that the cry of " Art for Art's sake," which
is being raised by those young men, and
which certainly isn't true for *them*, may be
true for *me*. What if henceforth I release
the winged steed of my recording art from
the obligation of dragging up the steep hill
of my inaptitude the dray filled with the
heavy goods which I have amassed in my
perhaps so mistaken desire for a respectably
weighty subject, and let the poor thing just
beautifully soar ? "

One perceives how far this mood had gone
with Mr James when the hero of *The Tragic
Muse* (1890) refuses a seat in Parliament
and the hand of a wealthy widow in order
that he might go on painting. From Mr
James, to whom marrying a widow appeared
as much superior to marrying a spinster
as privately acquiring a " piece " from the
dispersed collection of a deceased connois-
seur of repute is to buying old furniture
with no guarantee but one's own approval,
this was a portentous incident. And there
is vast significance in his sympathetic re-

presentation of Miriam Rooth, the young actress to whom the title refers, for before this period he would never have accepted the genius of the black-browed, untidy girl as an excuse for her lack of money and social position and manners. It had hitherto been his grimly expressed opinion that " the life of a woman is essentially an affair of private relations," and he had refused to dramatise in his imagination anything concerning women save their failures and successes as sexual beings ; which is like judging a cutlet not by its flavour, but by the condition of its pink-paper frill. That time had gone. He had abandoned all his prejudices in despair, and for many years to come was to show a divine charity, freely permitting every encountered thing to impress its essence on the receptive wax of his consciousness. For the next twelve years " impressions," as in his happy foreign childhood, " were not merely all right, but were the dearest things in the world."

IV

THE CRYSTAL BOWL

IN that octagonal room at the Prado, where each wall is an altar raised to beauty, because it is hung with pictures by Velasquez, in all the lesser works one finds some intimation of the grave, fine personality who produced all this wonder. At the sacred picture that was his first one says, " He was a pupil, and very proud of painting the old things better than the old men could, even though they meant nothing to him"; at the squat, black dwarfs, " He was so sure that the truth about the world was kind that he could look upon horror without fear " ; and at the sketches of the Villa Medici Gardens, " After hot, bleak Spain he loved Italy as one who has known passion loves a passionless girl." And the recreated personality, tangible enough to be liked, passes with one about the gallery

until suddenly, before the masterpieces, it
vanishes. With those it had nothing to do;
the thing that was his character, shaped out
of the innate traits of his dark stock by the
raw beauty of the land and the stiff rich life
of the court, brought him to the conception
of these works but lay sleeping through
their execution. When he was painting *Las
Hilanderas* he knew nothing save that the
weavers' flesh glowed golden in the dusty
sunlight of the factory; for the state of
genius consists of an utter surrender of the
mind to the subject. The artist at the
moment of creation must be like a saint
awaiting the embrace of God, scourging
appetite out of him, shrinking from sensa-
tion as though it were a sin, deleting self,
lifting his consciousness like an empty cup
to receive the heavenly draught.

And so, with the beginning of his second
period of genius, the reading of Mr James
ceased to give us the companionship of the
gentle, very pleasant American who seemed
homeless but quite serene, as though he were
tired of living in his boxes, but on the other

hand was very fond of travelling, that we
had grown to like in his books of the eighties.
He went away and sent no letter; but
instead, with a lavishness one would never
have suspected from his uneasy bearing,
sent a succession of jewels, great globed
jewels of experience, from which marvel-
lously conceived characters gave out their
milky gleams or fiery rays. The first tenta-
tive try at the mere impression, *The Aspern
Papers* (1888), gave an earnest of his gener-
osity. There one passes into the golden
glow of Venice, " where the sky and the sea
and the rosy air and the marble of the
palaces all shimmer and melt together. . . .
The gondola stopped, the old palace was
there. . . . How charming! it's grey and
pink!" And under the painted ceiling of
the old palace sits bleached and shrivelled
Juliana Bordereau, the memory of her love
affair with the great poet Aspern hanging
in the air like incense and filling the mind
with tears that such splendid lovers buy no
immortality, but grow old like the rest.
Above its mere amusing story the tale

breathes an elegy on the many good things
that are slain by age before death comes and
decently inters the body. For one watches,
with a kind of comic horror that such
grimaces should touch the face that Jeffery
Aspern kissed, the grin of senile irony with
which she meets the young American who
comes to wheedle her lover's letters out of
her, with which she wheedles money out of
him that she may provide for the future of
the poor spinster niece who moves tremu-
lously about her chair like a silly baaing
sheep; with which, one thinks, she possibly
anticipates the dreadful moment after her
death when the spinster dodderingly in-
forms the American that she could give him
her aunt's papers only " if you were a
relation . . . if you weren't a stranger. . . ."
Every drop of beauty is squeezed out of the
material by a pressure so cool and con-
trolled that, remembering how Benvenuto
Cellini " fell in his clothes and slept " after
he had taken similar small masterpieces from
the furnace, one waits for his exhaustion.
But it was given to Mr James, perhaps

because he was an American and so of a
stock oxygenated by contact with the free
airs of the new free lands, to swim longer n
the sea of perfection than any other writer.
It was not until fifteen years later, when
he was old and the disciples of the movement which had stimulated him all shabbily
dead, and talk about art locked away in a
dusty cupboard with the Japanese fans and
the blue china pots, that he turned tired and
came to shore.

He was sustained in this long swim by
two beloved subjects, one bitter and one
sweet. The literary life was written about
in those days almost as much as it was
talked about, and it was continually being
used by the young decadents as the occasion for predictions of their own later
squalor in which morphia and dark ladies,
moulded in the likeness of beautiful young
Mrs Patrick Campbell, played parts which
in the subsequent realisation were taken by
plain beer and plainer barmaids. Mr James
took up the poor, scribbled-about thing
and turned it over very reverently, none

knowing better than he that the artist was
the *sacer vates* of his time, and very sadly,
because he had now close on thirty years of
intimacy with artists behind him. He had
known Turgeniev, the most "beautiful
genius" of his age, and had found him
rather lonely and pre-eminently not eminent
in the eyes of the world; he had seen the
dark days of Rossetti; he had trod so close
on the heels of Alfred de Musset as to know
that *il s'absente trop de l'Académie parcequ'il
s'absinthe trop*; he had seen poor, fat little
Zola, who thought that though one could
not build Rome in a day one could describe
it in less, plodding and sweating up the
wrong road to art. And so, in a mood of
clear melancholy, with an occasional flash
of irony which was doubtless the sole com-
ment wrung from his urbanity by the fact
that that age, when the change of the
novel's price from thirty-one and sixpence to
six shillings had enormously increased the
reading public, had brought no enlargement
of his circle of readers, he wrote that
wonderful series of stories which began with

The Lesson of the Master (1888) and included
The Middle Years (1893), *The Next Time*
(1895), and *The Death of the Lion* (1894).
Save for that roaring joke, *The Coxon Fund*
(1894), where one sees Frank Saltram, a "free
rearrangement of Coleridge," charming
and sponging on the rich, bringing into their
drawing-rooms a swaying body that should
be taken home at once in a cab and a mind
" like a crystal suspended in the moral
world—swinging and shining and flashing
there," these are all sad stories. The
master is bullied out of being a master by
the financial importunities of a smart wife
and comely children; the author of *The
Middle Years* dies with none but an acquaint-
ance picked up at the seaside to hold his
hand; Ralph Limbert is killed by worry
because he could not stop producing masterpieces when it was the damned marketable
asset that was required to pay the wages of
his wife's maid; the lion dies in a cold
country house, with no fire in his bedroom,
while his hostess gets paragraphed for her
charity to the wild literary, and his last

manuscript goes astray downstairs somewhere between Lord Dorimont's man and
Lady Augusta's maid.   One knows next to
nothing at all about the faith consciously
rejected or adopted by Henry James, and
whether the atmosphere of speculative theo-
logy in which he was bred had made him
think religion as far beyond his mental range
as mathematics, or whether Christianity
seemed to him just the excuse of the Latin
races for building high cool places, very
grateful in the heat, and filling them with
incense and images of kind, interceding
people.   But in this melancholy series, and
indeed in all his later works—for right on
to *The Golden Bowl* (1905) he presents his
characters as being worthy of treatment just
because they are in some way or other
struggling to preserve some decency from
engulfment in the common lot of nastiness
—one perceives that he had been born with
the grim New England faith like a cold drop
in his blood.   The earth was a vale of tears,
and all one could do was to go on, unin-
fluenced by weeping or the fear of weeping,

to some high goal.   This sad belief, accompanied by so intense a consciousness that
his particular goal, the art of great writing,
was reached by a stonier and longer path
than any, might have been expected to provoke him rather to the fury of Landor or
the gloomy pomposity of Wordsworth than
to the unhurried, unimpassioned production
of these wonderful stories, these exquisite
vessels that swaggeringly hold and clearly
show the contained draught of truth, like
tall-stemmed goblets of Venetian glass.
But glass is the wrong image; for no hand
could ever break these, no critical eye detect
a crack.   They are so truthfully conceived
that one could compare them only to some
nobly infrangible substance, so realistic and
yet so charged with significance by their
fashioning that their likeness must be something which is transparent and yet gives the
light a white fire as it passed through.   It
is of crystal they are made, hard, luminous
crystal.

Mr James' second subject, which began
to show its white flowers in *The Other House*

(1896) and went on blossoming long after winter had fallen on his genius in *The Golden Bowl*, also showed him a son of New England. For it consists of nothing else than the demonstration, in varying and exquisitely selected circumstances, that blessed are the pure in heart; and that was certainly the beatitude that New England, with its fear of passion and publicity and its respect for spinsters and pastors of bleached lives, most regarded. Mr James demonstrated it in no spirit of moral propaganda, but for the technical reason that a situation is greatly elucidated if one of the persons engaged presents a consciousness like a polished silver surface, unobscured by any tracery of selfish preoccupations, which clearly mirrors the other participients and their movements. Perhaps he thereby discovered the real meaning of the beatitude, which may be no more than an expression of the obvious truth that he who receives the fullest impression of the world is likely to react most valuably to it. Certainly he invented a technical trick which in its way was as important as the discovery which Ibsen was making about the same time and which he himself used later in his last masterpiece, that if one had a really " great " scene one ought to leave it out and describe it simply by the full relation of its consequences. He showed that all sorts of things that are amusing enough to write about and are yet too ignoble for dignified art are lent the required nobility by being witnessed by grave candour; and that characters whose special claim is that they are " strange," but whose strangeness cannot be laboured by direct description lest they become crude, can have the gaps in their representation filled out by their effect on the simple. Rose Armiger, in *The Other House*, is made much more horrible because she exposes her dreadful passion before the simplicity of Tony Bream, just as a striped poisonous snake would seem more striped and poisonous if it flickered its black fang from an English rose-bush. The awfulness of Ida Farange, whose handsome appearance constituted " an abuse of visibility," of Beale Farange, whose vast scented beard was, since odd ladies liked to play with it, ultimately his chief source of income, would never have been important enough to be recorded if they had not formed a part of *What Maisie Knew* (1897); and the ensnarement of Sir Claude, her first step-parent, who was such a good fellow to talk to when his gaze didn't wander to the dark young woman in red who was sweeping into dinner or to the shining limbs of a Dieppe fishwife, by the beautiful, genteel young trollop who was her second step-parent, would have been a matter too *louche* for representation if Maisie had not so beautifully cared for him. The battle over *The Spoils of Poynton* (1897), where the greedy mother tries to defend the fine " things " of her dead husband's house from her imbecile son's vulgar bride, would be too unrelievedly a history of greed to be borne were not exquisite Fleda Vetch in the foreground, being fond of the mother, loving the son. The best ghost story in the world, *The Turn of the Screw* (1898), is the more ghostly because the apparitions of the valet

and the governess, appearing at the
dangerous place, the top of the tower on the
other side of the lake, that they may tempt
the children they corrupted in their lives to
join them in their eternal torment, are seen
by the clear eyes of the honourable and fear-
less lady who tells the tale. And *In the
Cage* (1898) has no subject but the purity
of the romantic little telegraphist who sits
behind the wire netting at the grocer's.
Her heart is like a well of clear water,
through which, when the handsome Guards-
man comes in to send a telegram to his
mistress, love strikes down like a shaft of
light.

One pauses, horrified to find oneself ticking off these masterpieces on one's fingers,
as though they were so many books by Mrs
Humphry Ward or buns by Lyons. And
yet what can one do ? Criticism must break
down when it comes to masterpieces. For
if one is creative one wants to go away and
spend oneself utterly on this sacred business
of creation, wring out of oneself every drop
of this inestimable thing art; and if one is

not creative one can only put out a tremulous finger to touch the marvellous shining crystal, and be silent with wonder. Deep wonder, since these are not, as fools have pretended, merely rich treatments of the trivial. For although he could not grasp a complicated abstraction, was teased by the implications of a great cause, and angered by an idea that could be understood only by the synthesis of many references, he could dive down serenely, like a practised diver going under the sea for pearls, into the twilit depths of the heart to seize his secrets. There is in humanity an instinct for ritual, there lies in all of us a desire to commemorate our deep emotions, that would otherwise glow in our bosoms and die down for ever, by some form that adds to the beauty of the world; but there is only one expression of it in literature that is not poisonously silly. Newman and the Tractarians and Monsignor Benson make the ritualist seem as big a fool as the old woman who carries a potato in her pocket to ward off rheumatism. Sabatier makes him seem the kind of

person who takes sugar in his tea, paints in
water-colour and likes *The Roadmender*.
But there is a story by Henry James called
The Altar of the Dead, rejected again and
again by the caste of cretins who edit the
magazines and reviews of this unhappy
country, although of so perfect a beauty
that one can read every separate paragraph
every day of one's life for the music of the
sentences and the loveliness of the presented images, which takes ritual from the
trembling hands of the coped old men and
exhibits it as something that those who love
the natural frame of things and hate super-
stition need not fear to accept. It tells
how an ageing man acquires an altar in a
Roman Catholic church and burns at it
candles to his many dead, and by worship-
ping there keeps so close company with their
charity and sweetness that, at his end, the
blaze of white lights inspires him to a last
supreme act of forgiveness to an enemy;
and the beautiful recital makes one's mind
no longer fear to admit that the splendour
of a Cathedral Mass may, although one's

unbelief fly like an arrow through the show and transfix even the Cross itself, fulfil a noble need. Once at least Henry James poured into his crystal goblet the red wine that nourishes the soul.

And it held, too, a liberal draught of the least trivial distillation of man's mind, which is tragedy, in *The Wings of the Dove* (1902). That story is the perfect example of what he had declared in *The Tragic Muse* the artistic performance should always be: " the application, clear and calculated, crystal-firm, as it were, of the idea conceived in the glow of experience, of suffering, of joy." For Milly Theale, the American heiress, " who had arts and idiosyncrasies of which no great account could have been given, but which were a daily grace if you lived with them; such as the art of being almost tragically impatient and yet making it light as air; of being inexplicably sad and yet making it clear as noon; of being unmistakably sad and yet making it soft as dusk," whose hopeful progress through Europe stops suddenly at the dark portal

in Harley Street, is but the ghost of Mary
Temple, whose death thirty years before
had been felt by Henry and William James
as the end of their youth. All those years
he had held in his heart the memory of that
poor girl, " conscious of a great capacity for
life, but early stricken and doomed, con-
demned to die under short respite while also
enamoured of the world; aware, moreover, of
the condemnation and passionately desiring
to ' put in' before extinction as many of the
finer vibration as possible and so achieve,
however briefly and brokenly, the sense of
having lived"; but with the prescience of
the artist he had delayed until he had per-
fected his art to undertake the heavy task of
presenting her tragedy without mitigation
and yet making it bearable and beautiful.
Then he lavished his technical resources on
her history as he might have laid flowers on
her grave. There is nothing more miracu-
lous in all his works than the way he con-
trives that, when her agony becomes too
great to be directly represented and has to
be suggested by its effect upon others, he

yet breaks no link of the intimacy between
the reader and his heroine, but provides
that her increasing physical absence shall
be so compensated for by her spiritual
presence that her rare appearances are like
long-expected visits from a distant friend.
One's knowledge of her glows into love when
one sees her holding a reception in the faded
golden splendours of the Venetian palace to
which she has dragged herself to die, smiling
bravely at her guests, bidding musicians
strike up to keep them gay, playing, to preserve her hands from any gesture of anguish
or appearance of lassitude, with the rope
of pearls that seems to weigh down her
wasted body. Yet one gets one's vision
through the hard, envious eyes of Kate
Croy, who is the hawk circling over the poor
dying dove, and the appalled gaze of Merton
Densher, Kate's secret lover, whom she has
trapped into a profession of love for Milly
so that the deluded girl will leave him her
fortune. And one sees her most radiantly
of all in the interview which she grants to
Densher when she has discovered the cruel

fraud practised on her and is dying of the knowledge, although one is told no more than that " she received me just as usual, in that glorious great *salone*, in the dress she always wears, from her inveterate corner of her sofa." From the love it lit in his heart, a love so great that for very shame Kate cannot marry him even when her machinations have achieved complete success at Milly's death, one perceives that this was the dying girl's assumption, that her sweetness and strength must at that hour have flowered so divinely that the skies opened and they were no longer matter for a human history. But about this masterpiece, too, there can be nothing said. One just sits and looks up, while the Master lifts his old grief, changed by his craftsmanship into eternal beauty as the wafer is changed to the Host by the priest's liturgy, enclosed from decay, prisoned in perfection, in the great shining crystal bowl of his art.

V

THE GOLDEN BOWL

THE signs of age appeared in Mr James' work like white streaks in a black beard; between two vital and vigorous books there would appear one that in its garrulity and complacent surrender to mannerism predicted decay. It became clear, first of all, that he was no longer able to bear up with serenity under his deep sense that life was a vale of tears. How much he wished it would all stop is manifest in that strangest of all visions of Paradise, *The Great Good Place* (1900). We all have our hopes of what gifts the hereafter may bring us, and in most cases we desire some compensation for the limitations of our human knowledge; we promise ourselves that when we lean over the gold bar of heaven a competent angel will bustle up, clasping innumerable divinely clear text-

books under its wings, to tell us absolutely
everything about physics, with special reference to the movements of the heavenly
bodies spinning below.   But it is the essence
of Mr James' Paradise that there is nothing
there at all but a climate, a sweet soft
climate in which the most that happens is
one of those summer sprinkles that brings
out smells.   This fatigue of life, this hunger
for the peace of nothingness, showed itself
in his increasing preference for laying the
scene of his novels in the great good places
of this earth, where there is nothing more
dangerous in the parks and on the terraces
than deer and peacocks, and nothing more
disturbing to the soul in the high rooms
and interminable galleries than well-bred
women.   It was not a gain to his art; under
its influence he committed the twittering
over teacups which compose the collection
of short stories called *The Better Sort*
(1903), and the incidentally beautiful but
devastatingly artificial *The Awkward Age*
(1899), in which the reader is perpetually
confused because Nanda Brookenham, one

of the most charming of Mr James' " pure
in heart," is wept over as though she had
been violated body and soul, when all that
has happened is that she has been brought
up in a faster set than the world thinks
desirable for a young unmarried girl.   And
it was peculiarly unfortunate that, while his
subjects grew flimsier and his settings more
impressive, his style became more and more
elaborate. With sentences vast as the
granite blocks of the Pyramids and a scene
that would have made a site for a capital
he set about constructing a story the size of
a hen-house.   The type of these unhappier
efforts of Mr James' genius is *The Sacred
Fount* (1901), where, with a respect for the
mere gross largeness and expensiveness of
the country house which almost makes one
write the author Mr Jeames, he records
how a week-end visitor spends more intellectual force than Kant can have used
on *The Critique f Pure Reason* in an
unsuccessful attempt to discover whether
there exists between certain of his fellow-
guests a relationship not more interesting

among these vacuous people than it is among sparrows. The finely wrought descriptions of the leisured life make one feel as though one sat in a beautiful old castle, granting its beauty but not pleased, because one is a prisoner, while the small, mean story worries one like a rat nibbling at the wainscot. One takes it as significant that the unnamed host and hostess of the party never appear save to " give signals." The tiny, desperate figures this phrase shows to the mind's eye, semaphoring to each other across incredibly extended polished vistas to keep up their courage under these looming, soaring vaults, may be taken as symbols of the heart and intellect which Mr James had now forgotten in his elaboration of their social envelope.

But with this method, as in every form of literary activity save only playwriting, in which he was rather worse than Sidney Grundy in much the same way, Mr James gained his radiant triumphs. There could be nothing more trivial than the *donnée* of *The Ambassadors* (1903) ; there is no dignity

or significance in the situation of Lambert
Strether, an American who is engaged, in
that odd way common to Mr James' characters, to a woman whom he certainly does
not love and hardly seems to like, and goes
at her bidding to Paris to cut her cubbish
son clear from an entanglement with a
Frenchwoman. And yet so artfully is the
tale displayed in the setting of lovely, clean,
white Paris and green France, lifting her
poplars into the serene strong light of the
French sky, that the reader holds his breath
over the story of how Strether " had come
with a view that might have been figured by
a clear, green liquid, say, in a neat glass
phial; and the liquid, once poured into the
open cup of *application*, once exposed to the
action of another air, had begun to turn from
green to red, or whatever, and might, for all
he knew, be on its way to purple, to black,
to yellow "; how, in fact, the old " international situation " acted on the new generation of Americans. But that book is not
typical of this period, for it is singularly free
from those great sentences which sprawl

over the pages of *The Golden Bowl* with such
an effect of rank vegetable growth that one
feels that if one took cuttings of them one
could raise a library in the garden.   And it
is those sentences which absorb, at the last,
the whole of Mr James' attention.

For he ceased, as time went on, to pay any
attention to the emotional values of his
stories; it is one of the strangest things
about *The Golden Bowl* that the frame
on which there hangs the most elaborate
integument of suggestion and exposition
ever woven by the mind of man is an ugly
and incompletely invented story about
some people who are sexually mad.   Adam
Verver, an American millionaire, buys an
Italian prince for his daughter Maggie, and
in her turn she arranges a marriage between
her father and Charlotte, her school friend,
because she thinks he may be lonely without
her.   And although it is plain that people
who buy " made-up " marriages are more
awful than the admittedly awful people
who buy " made-up " ties, they are presented to one as vibrating exquisitely to

every fine chord of life, as thinking about
each other with the anxious subtlety of
lovers, as so steeped in a sense of one another
that they invent a sea of poetic phrases,
beautiful images, discerning metaphors that
break on the reader's mind like the unceas-
ing surf.   And when one tries to discover
from the recorded speeches of these people
whether there was no palliation of their
ugly circumstances one finds that the
dialogue, usually so compact a raft for the
conveyance of the meaning of Mr James'
novels, has been smashed up on this sea
of phrases and drifts in, a plank at a time,
on the copious flood :

"Maggie happened to learn, by some
other man's greeting of him, in the bright
Roman way, from a street corner as we
passed, that one of the Prince's baptismal
names, the one always used for him among
his relations, was Amerigo ; which—as you
probably don't know, however, even after
a lifetime of *me*—was the name, four
hundred years ago, or whenever, of the
pushing man who followed, across the sea,

in the wake of Columbus and succeeded, where Columbus had failed, in becoming godfather, or name-father, to the new continent; so the thought of any connection with him can even now thrill our artless breasts."

And as if it was not enough that these people should say literally unspeakable sentences like that, and do incredible things, the phrases make them do things which they never did. For the metaphors are so beautifully and completely presented to the mind that it retains them as having as real and physical an existence as the facts. When we learn that the relationship between Charlotte and the Prince had reared itself in Maggie's life like " some wonderful, beautiful, but outlandish pagoda, a structure plated with hard, bright porcelain, coloured and figured and adorned, at the overhanging eaves, with silver bells that tinkled ever so charmingly, when stirred by chance airs," and the simile is cunningly developed for seven or eight hundred words, one is left with a confused impression that a pagoda formed part of the furniture at Portland Place and that Maggie oddly elected to keep her husband inside it. And to cap it all these people are not even human, for their thoughts concerning their relationships are so impassioned and so elaborate that they can never have had either energy or time for the consideration of anything else in the world. A race of creatures so inveterately specialist as Maggie Verver could never have attained man's mastery over environment, but would still be specialising on the cocoa-nut or some such simple form of diet.

Decidedly *The Golden Bowl* is not good as a novel; but what it is supremely good as can be discovered when one learns how, in these later days, Mr James used to compose his novels. He began by dictating a short draft which, even in the case of such a cartload of apes and ivory as *The Golden Bowl*, might be no longer than thirty thousand words. Then he would take this draft in his hand and would dictate it all over again with what he intended to be enlightening additions, but which, since the mere act of talking set all his family on to something quite different from the art of letters, made it less and less of a novel. For the James family had, as was shown by their father's many reported phrases, by William James' charm as a lecturer, and by the social greatness of Robertson James, a genius for conversation. For long years it had remained latent in Henry James, who had in youth suffered much from that stockishness which often comes to those who are burning all their energy for creative purposes and have none left for personal display; but latterly it had been liberated by the consciousness of maturity and fame. At last it became a passion with him, and he decided to converse, not only with his friends, but with his public. This was bad for his novels, so long as one considered them as such, since a novel should be the presentation and explanation of a subject while a conversation is a fantasia of entertaining phrases on themes the essentials of which are to some extent already in the possession of the interlocutors. But once one considers them as a flow of bright things said about people Mr James knows and that one rather thinks one has met, but is not quite sure, one perceives that the crystal bowl of Mr James' art was not, as one had feared, broken. He had but gilded its clear sides with the gold of his genius for phrase-making, and now, instead of lifting it with a priest-like gesture to exhibit a noble subject, held it on his knees as a treasured piece of bric-à-brac and tossed into it, with an increasing carelessness, any sort of subject—a jewel, a rose, a bit of string, a visiting-card—confident that the surrounding golden glow would lend it beauty. Indiscriminately he dropped into it his precious visions of his revisited motherland, in *The American Scene* (1907); the dry little anecdotes of *The Finer Grain* (1910); the tittering triviality of *The Outcry* (1911); and his judgment of his own works in the prefaces to the New York edition of the *Novels and Tales of Henry James* (1908-1909).

Always it was good, rambling talk, although fissured now and then with an old man's lapses into tiresomeness, when he split hairs until there were no longer any hairs to split and his mental gesture became merely the making of agitated passes over a complete baldness.

And here and there the prose achieves a beauty of its own; but it is no longer the beauty of a living thing, but rather the " made" beauty which bases its claims to admiration chiefly on its ingenuity, like those crystal clocks with jewelled works and figures moving as the hours chimed, which were the glory of mediæval palaces.

William James died in 1910, and Henry James, who had already begun to savour the bitterness of outliving brothers and friends and pets, whiled away the next few years of separation from his adored brother in the composition of two beautiful books about their childhood and youth, *A Small Boy* (1913), and *Notes of a Son and Brother* (1914), and a third autobiographical volume which is not yet published. Then came the European War, in which he enlisted as a spiritual soldier. By innumerable beautiful acts, by kindly visits to French and Belgian refugees and wounded soldiers, by gifts of money and writings to war charities, he raised an altar to the dead who had died for the countries which he had always loved at the hands of the country which, ever since he was a student at Bonn, he had always loathed. In July, 1915, he took the great step, fraught for him with the deepest emotions, of renouncing his American citizenship and becoming a naturalised British subject; and in January, 1916, he did England the further honour of accepting the Order of Merit. And on 28th February, 1916, he died, leaving the white light of his genius to shine out for the eternal comfort of the mind of man.

A SHORT BIBLIOGRAPHY OF MR HENRY JAMES' PRINCIPAL WORKS

[A complete bibliography of the works of Mr James would
form a much thicker volume than this book. A
useful bibliography up to 1906, compiled by Mr
Frederick Allen King, is included as an appendix in
Miss Elisabeth Luther Cary's *The Novels of Henry
James* (Putnam); and a complete bibliography
covering the same period, which gives an interesting
list of his early unsigned contributions to periodicals,
has been compiled by Mr Leroy Phillips and published
by Messrs Constable. The following bibliography
records only the first editions of publications in book
form.]

The American (*Ward, Lock*). 1877.

French Poets and Novelists (*Macmillan*). **1878.**

The Europeans (*Macmillan*). 1878.

Roderick Hudson (*Macmillan*). 1879.

Daisy Miller. An International Episode. **Four Meetings**
  (*Macmillan*). 1879.

The Madonna of the Future. Longstaff's Marriage.
  Madame de Mauves. Eugene Pickering. The Diary
  of a Man of Fifty. Benvolio (*Macmillan*). 1879.

Hawthorne (*Macmillan*). Included in English Men of
  Letters Series, edited by John Morley. 1879.

Confidence (*Chatto & Windus*). 1880.

Washington Square. The Pension Beaurepas. A Bundle
  of Letters (*Macmillan*). 1881.

The Portrait of a Lady (*Macmillan*). 1881.

Portraits of Places (*Macmillan*). 1883.

Tales of Three Cities : The Impressions of a Cousin. Lady Barbarina. A New England Winter (*Macmillan*). 1884.

Stories Revived: Vol. I. The Author of Beltraffio. Pandora. The Path of Duty. A Day of Days. A Light Man. Vol. II. Georgina's Reasons. A Passionate Pilgrim. A Landscape Painter. Rose-Agathe. Vol. III. Poor Richard. The Last of the Valerii. Master Eustace. The Romance of Certain Old Clothes. A Most Extraordinary Case (*Macmillan*). 1885.

The Bostonians (*Macmillan*). 1886.

The Princess Casamassima (*Macmillan*). 1886.

The Reverberator (*Macmillan*). 1888.

The Aspern Papers. Louisa Pallant. The Modern Warning (*Macmillan*). 1888.

Partial Portraits (*Macmillan*). 1888.

A London Life. The Patagonia. The Liar. Mrs Temperley (*Macmillan*). 1889.

The Tragic Muse (*Macmillan*). 1890.

The Lesson of the Master. The Marriages. The Pupil. Brooksmith. The Solution. Sir Edmund Orme (*Macmillan*). 1892.

The Real Thing. Sir Dominick Ferrand. Nona Vincent. The Chaperon. Greville Fane (*Macmillan*). 1893.

The Private Life. The Wheel of Time. Lord Beaupré. The Visits. Collaboration. Owen Wingrave (*Osgood, McIlvaine*). 1893.

Essays in London (*Osgood, McIlvaine*). 1893.

Theatricals : Two Comedies. Tenants. Disengaged (*Osgood, McIlvaine*). 1894.

Theatricals : Second Series. The Album. The Reprobate (*Osgood, McIlvaine*). 1895.

BIBLIOGRAPHY

Terminations : The Death of the Lion.   The Coxon Fund.
The Middle Years.   The Altar of the Dead (*Heine-mann*).   1895.

Embarrassments : The Figure in the Carpet.   Glasses.   The
Next Time.   The Way it Came (*Heinemann*) 1896.

The Other House (*Heinemann*).   1896.

The Spoils of Poynton (*Heinemann*).   1897.

What Maisie Knew (*Heinemann*).   1897.

In the Cage (*Duckworth*).   1898.

The Two Magics.   The Turn of the Screw.   Covering End
(*Macmillan*).   1898.

The Awkward Age (*Heinemann*).   1899.

The Soft Side : The Great Good Place.   " Europe."
Paste.   The Real Right Thing.   The Great Condition.
The Tree of Knowledge.   The Abasement of the
Northmores.   The Given Case.   John Delavoy.   The
Third Person.   Maud-Evelyn.   Miss Gunton of
Poughkeepsie (*Methuen*).   1900.

The Sacred Fount (*Methuen*).   1901.

The Wings of the Dove (*Constable*).   1902.

The Better Sort : Broken Wings.   The Beldonald Hol-bein.   The Two Faces.   The Tone of Time.   The
Special Type.   Mrs Medwin.   Flickerbridge.   The
Story in It.   The Beast in the Jungle.   The Birth-place.   The Papers (*Methuen*).   1903.

The Ambassadors (*Methuen*).   1903.

William Wetmore Story and his Friends (*Blackwood*).
1903.

The Golden Bowl (*Methuen*).   1905.

English Hours (*Heinemann*).   1905.

The American Scene (*Chapman & Hall*).   1907.

Italian Hours (*Heinemann*).   1909.

The Finer Grain : The Velvet Glove.   Mora Montravers.
A Round of Visits.   Crapy Cornelia.   The Bench of
Desolation (*Methuen*).   1910.

The Outcry (*Methuen*). 1911.

A Small Boy (*Macmillan*). 1913.

Notes of a Son and Brother (*Macmillan*). 1914.

Notes on Novelists (*Dent*). 1914.

A Collection of Novels and Tales by Henry James was published by Messrs Macmillan in 1883. This consisted of reprints of The Portrait of a Lady, Roderick Hudson, The American, Washington Square, The Europeans, Confidence, Madame de Mauves, An International Episode, The Pension Beaurepas, Daisy Miller, Four Meetings, Long-staff's Marriage, Benvolio, The Madonna of the Future, A Bundle of Letters, The Diary of a Man of Fifty, and Eugene Pickering ; and two stories, The Siege of London and The Point of View, which had not before been published in England.

The New York Edition of the Novels and Tales of Mr Henry James was published by Messrs Macmillan during 1908-1909. Each novel and each volume of short stories has a critical preface by the author, and each volume has a photograph by Alvin Langdon Coburn as frontispiece. The following is the order :—

1. Roderick Hudson. 2. The American. 3, 4. The Portrait of a Lady. 5, 6. The Princess Casamassima. 7, 8. The Tragic Muse. 9. The Awkward Age. 10. The Spoils of Poynton ; A London Life ; The Chaperon. 11. What Maisie Knew ; In the Cage ; The Pupil. 12. The Aspern Papers ; The Turn of the Screw ; The Liar ; The Two Faces. 13. The Reverberator ; Madame de Mauves ; A Passionate Pilgrim ; The Madonna of the Future ; Louisa Pallant. 14. Lady Barbarina ; The Siege of London ; An International Episode ; The Pension Beaurepas ; A Bundle of Letters ; The Point of View. 15. The Lesson of the Master ; The Death of the Lion ;

The Next Time; The Figure in the Carpet; The Coxon Fund. 16. The Author of Beltraffio; The Middle Years; Greville Fane; Broken Wings; The Tree of Knowledge; The Abasement of the Northmores; The Great Good Place; Four Meetings; Paste; Europe; Miss Gunton of Poughkeepsie; Fordham Castle. 17. The Altar of the Dead; The Beast in the Jungle; The Birthplace; The Private Life; Owen Wingrave; The Friends of the Friends; Sir Edmund Orme; The Real Right Thing; The Jolly Corner; Julia Bride. 18. Daisy Miller; Pandora; The Patagonia; The Marriages; The Real Thing; Brooksmith; The Beldonald Holbein; The Story in It; Flickerbridge; Mrs Medwin. 19, 20. The Ambassadors. 21, 22. The Wings of the Dove. 23, 24. The Golden Bowl.

Fordham Castle, The Jolly Corner and Julia Bride had not previously been published. All the early works have been subjected to a revision which in several cases, notably Daisy Miller and Four Meetings, amounts to their ruin.

AMERICAN BIBLIOGRAPHY

[When the contents of collections of short stories have
    been given in full in the English bibliography they
    are entered here by their title only.]

A Passionate Pilgrim and Other Tales: The Last of the
    Valerii. Eugene Pickering. The Madonna of the
    Future. The Romance of Certain Old Clothes.
    Madame de Mauves (*James R. Osgood*; present pub-
    lisher, *Houghton, Mifflin*). 1875.

Transatlantic Sketches: Articles reprinted from *The
    Nation, The Atlantic Monthly*, and *The Galaxy*
    (*James R. Osgood*; present publishers, *Houghton,
    Mifflin*). 1875.

Roderick Hudson (*James R. Osgood*; present publisher,
    Houghton, Mifflin). 1876.

The American (*James R. Osgood*; present publisher,
    Houghton, Mifflin). 1877.

Watch and Ward (*Houghton, Osgood*; present publisher,
    Houghton, Mifflin). 1878.

The Europeans (*Houghton, Osgood*; present publisher,
    Houghton, Mifflin). 1878.

Daisy Miller (*Harper*). 1878.

An International Episode (*Harper*). 1878.

Hawthorne (*Harper*). 1880.

The Diary of a Man of Fifty and A Bundle of Letters
    (*Harper*). 1880.

Confidence (*Houghton, Osgood*; present publisher, *Houghton
    Mifflin*). 1880.

Washington Square. Illustrated by George du Maurier
    (*Harper*). 1881.

The Portrait of a Lady (*Houghton, Mifflin*). 1881.

BIBLIOGRAPHY

Daisy Miller : A Comedy. Privately printed. 1882.

The Siege of London, The Pension Beaurepas, and The Point of View (*James R. Osgood* ; present publisher, *Houghton, Mifflin*). 1883.

Portraits of Places (*James R. Osgood* ; present publisher, *Houghton, Mifflin*). 1883.

Tales of Three Cities (*James R. Osgood* ; present publisher, *Houghton, Mifflin*). 1884.

A Little Tour in France (*James R. Osgood* ; present publisher, *Houghton, Mifflin*). 1884.

The Author of Beltraffio. Pandora. Georgina's Reasons. The Path of Duty. Four Meetings (*James R. Osgood* ; present publisher, *Houghton, Mifflin*). 1885.

The Bostonians (*Macmillan*). 1886.

The Princess Casamassima (*Macmillan*). 1886.

The Reverberator (*Macmillan*). 1888.

The Aspern Papers (*Macmillan*). 1888.

Partial Portraits (*Macmillan*). 1888.

A London Life (*Macmillan*). 1889.

The Tragic Muse (*Houghton, Mifflin*). 1890.

The Lesson of the Master (*Macmillan*). 1892.

The Real Thing (*Macmillan*). 1893.

The Private Life. Lord Beaupré. The Visits (*Harper*). 1893.

The Wheel of Time. Collaboration. Owen Wingrave (*Harper*). 1893.

Picture and Text. Essays on Art (*Harper*). 1893.

Essays in London (*Harper*). 1893.

Theatricals (*Harper*). 1894.

Theatricals : Second Series (*Harper*). 1895.

Terminations (*Harper*). 1895.

Embarrassments (*Macmillan*). 1896.

The Other House (*Macmillan*). 1896.

The Spoils of Poynton (*Houghton, Mifflin*). 1897.

What Maisie Knew (*Herbert S. Stone*). 1897.

In the Cage (*Herbert S. Stone*). 1898.
The Two Magics (*Macmillan*). 1898.
The Awkward Age (*Harper*). 1899.
The Soft Side (*Macmillan*). 1900.
The Sacred Fount (*Scribner's*). 1901.
The Wings of the Dove (*Scribner's*). 1902.
The Better Sort (*Scribner's*). 1903.
The Ambassadors (*Harper*). 1903.
William Wetmore Story (*Houghton, Mifflin*). 1903.
The Golden Bowl (*Scribner's*). 1904.
English Hours (*Houghton, Mifflin*). 1905.
The Question of our Speech. The Lesson of Balzac
    (*Houghton, Mifflin*). 1905.
The American Scene (*Harper*). 1907.
Italian Hours (*Houghton, Mifflin*). 1909.
The Finer Grain (*Scribner's*). 1910.
The Outcry (*Scribner's*). 1911.
A Small Boy (*Scribner's*). 1913.
Notes of a Son and Brother (*Scribner's*). 1914.
Notes on Novelists (*Scribner's*). 1914.

The New York Edition of the Novels and Tales of
Mr Henry James was published in America by Messrs
Scribner's Sons.

INDEX

DATE DUE

DEC 11 1973		
5-3-28		
5/20/83		
APR 17 1983		
MAR 24 2000		
GAYLORD		PRINTED IN U.S.A.